Volcano!

Dome of Fire

by Barbara Bondar

Perfection Learning®

Cover Photograph: NOAA
Inside Illustration: Brian Brombaugh
Larry Nolte
Kay Ewald

Volcano photos courtesy of National Oceanic and Atmospheric Administration unless otherwise noted.

About the Author

Barbara Bondar is a specialist in interdisciplinary learning and psycholinguistics (which is pretty heavy). She is the author of over 20 highly praised educational books published in the United States and Canada (which means she gets around some). Her last book for children, *On the Shuttle; eight days in space,* won the 1994 Information Book of the Year Award from the Children's Literature Roundtables.

She has also written and hosted educational television programs and taught film animation to exceptional students. A master teacher, university lecturer, materials reviewer, comic book fiend, and data program analyst, Bondar recently wrote her first interactive computer game for kids of all ages.

She is thankful to be alive at a time when scientists have learned enough about volcanoes that she doesn't have to worry about being a human sacrifice to stop an eruption somewhere.

When she is not writing, she offers multimedia presentations to students at all levels on different subjects and motivational presentations to teachers at educational conferences just about anywhere. Check her out at *writebiz.com.*

Table of Contents

March 27, 1986, eruption at Augustine, Alaska

CHAPTER 1

Not Just a Pretty Mountain

The Where and Why of Volcanoes

Imagine   It is 79 A.D. You are in total darkness because of falling **ash.** You can't see your parents. The ground is shaking under your feet. All you can hear is the growling mountain. The smell of rotten eggs makes you ill.

The fallen ash against the door rises. It's up to your knees.

People pass you. Their lanterns shine dimly. Your eyes sting from the fumes and the hot dust. You have trouble breathing. You are alone. Except for your dog shivering at your feet.

What is happening?

Is this the Day of Judgment? Is it Vulcan, the god of fire? Is he inside the mountain making swords for the gods? Or is he angry because you spoke rudely to your parents?

What should you do?

Should you look for your family? But it's so hard to see.

Should you race for the harbor? You might find safety on a boat.

Should you run along the shore away from the mountain? You might find safety there.

You must choose wisely. Or you could die.

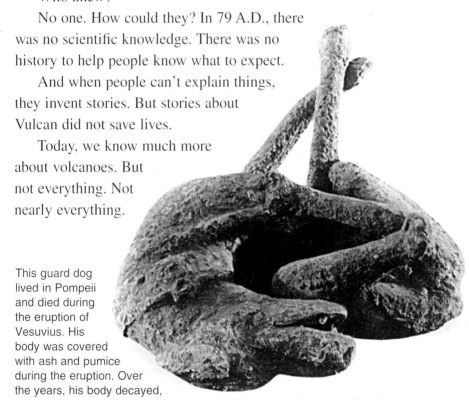

If this is 79 A.D., Vesuvius, the great killer volcano, is erupting.

Luckily, many people chose wisely. They left when their beautiful mountain showed no sign of stopping after a few hours.

But others didn't. They stayed. And they died the next morning. Choked by the fumes. Or crushed as roofs fell in under the weight of ash and cinders. The city of Pompeii was buried under 20 feet of ash.

Who knew?

No one. How could they? In 79 A.D., there was no scientific knowledge. There was no history to help people know what to expect.

And when people can't explain things, they invent stories. But stories about Vulcan did not save lives.

Today, we know much more about volcanoes. But not everything. Not nearly everything.

This guard dog lived in Pompeii and died during the eruption of Vesuvius. His body was covered with ash and pumice during the eruption. Over the years, his body decayed, and the ash and pumice hardened to rock. The shape from his body left a hollow in the rock. Scientists filled the hollow with wet plaster to get this form. Note his collar.

A Lot of Crust

For hundreds of years, people have studied the continents. They are like pieces of a monster-sized jigsaw puzzle.

Find a world map. Cut out the continents carefully. Play around with their fit.

Scientists have proven that the continents once fit together. But how did this land mass move apart?

Inside Story

This is how we think the earth works.

Think of the earth as a huge ball with layers. The **core** (inner and outer) of the earth is solid. It's under the pressure of a lot of weight. That's why it stays solid.

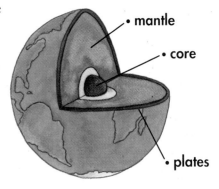

The **mantle** is the next layer. It's like the cheese in a grilled-cheese sandwich.

The crust is the outer layer. This thin layer is broken into great pieces called **plates**.

The plates float like giant rafts on the mantle. They are always moving.

Major Action

Where the plates move apart, a **rift** is formed. Most rifts are on the seafloor.

One of the largest rift zones is in the middle of the Atlantic Ocean. Here plates are always moving apart.

Hot, melted rock beneath the crust of the earth is called **magma**. Magma rises in the rifts. As the magma rises, it cools and becomes part of the seafloor.

The continuing action in the seafloor slowly pushes the continents apart. How slowly? At the speed your fingernails grow! Not fast. You can't feel it. But give it enough time, and it adds up to the width of an ocean!

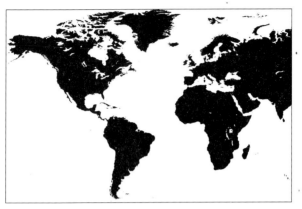

Major Meltdown

Plates also collide. The ocean plates are the oldest, heaviest, and coldest parts of the crust. When they bump and grind into plates of dry land, they sink back into the mantle.

Where the edge of a plate sinks beneath another plate, it heats up and begins to melt. The heat can produce a series of volcano islands like Japan. Or a series of volcano mountains like those on the west coasts of North and South America.

Try this. Rub one hand under the other. Do you feel heat?

This is what happens when one of the earth's plates rubs under another! So much heat is produced that the earth underneath melts—land, sand, rock, and soil. Magma is formed.

What happens to all that melted rock (magma)?

Major Moves

Since it is so hot, magma is lighter than the surrounding rock. It pushes and pokes its way upward.

When the magma escapes, it is called **lava**. A volcano is formed. If a volcano already exists, it comes to life. Hundreds of volcanoes lie around the edges of plates all over the earth.

Volcanic action spreads and builds the seafloor. This action spits out enough magma to grow an island as big as Iceland. Volcanic action causes mountains like Vesuvius to explode.

By spreading and sinking, earth recycles itself. New crust for old.

Major Meteors

Volcanoes also form over **hot spots.** Scientists think hot spots were caused by **meteorites** hitting the earth. The impact cracked the plate and damaged the mantle below.

So today, the magma bubbles up under each hot spot, like a giant blowtorch.

Hawaii is over a hot spot. The hot spot under Hawaii has left a trail of islands. They run north and west from Hawaii to the Aleutian Islands.

Hawaiian Islands

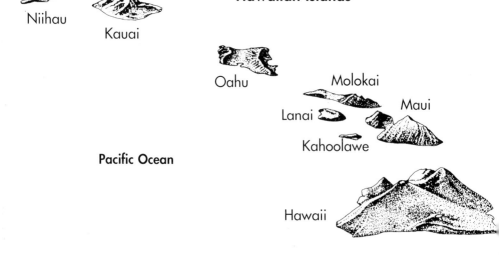

Niihau

Kauai

Oahu

Molokai

Lanai

Maui

Kahoolawe

Pacific Ocean

Hawaii

These islands are actually the tops of underwater mountains! Many of the mountains didn't make it to the surface of the ocean. All this island building has taken millions of years.

Ring of Fire

The plates surrounding the Pacific Ocean have many active volcanoes. This area is known as the **Ring of Fire**. About 75% of land volcanoes grow here.

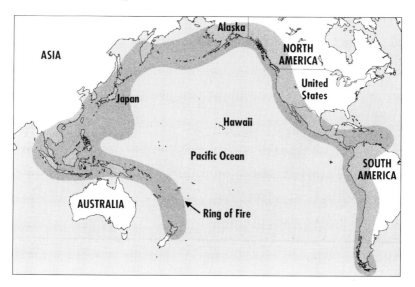

Space Eyes

Space offers a great view of the trail of volcanoes. For over 30 years, NASA has taken photos of volcano sites around the world.

 Famous Thinker

In the early 1900s, Arthur Holmes, a Scottish geologist, was the first to explain continental drift. He suggested that slow-moving heat currents from the mantle move earth's plates. It was not until the 1960s that other scientists picked up on the idea.

CHAPTER 2

Smoke Signals

When Earth Rumbles

Imagine You are wearing sandals, shorts, and a T-shirt. It's hot. You're sweating as you work with your family.

You twist and turn two long, sturdy wooden poles into the ground. You use them to pry up a slab of salt. Then your father hacks the slab of salt with his ax. Your mother and brother work beside you.

Later, you help load the salt into burlap sacks. The sacks are piled beside your father's camel. At the end of the day, your family will have much salt to sell.

You wonder how all this salt got here. It's all around as far as your eyes can see.

Just two miles away, there are small salt cones no taller than your knee. They gurgle brine and foul-smelling bright yellow sulfur.

This is the north end of a very long valley. In the valley, there are volcanoes, huge cracks in the ground, and earthquakes. There are lakes that stretch and lands that heave.

Your teacher says it's a dangerous place to live. But you haven't seen any danger. Plus, a little danger would be exciting.

Unfortunately, your parents won't let you wander too far.

They worry that the earth might open up and swallow you. But you plan to check it out.

What might you find?

You'll find that you are at the top of Africa's Great Rift Valley. You are standing on a seafloor spreading on dry land!

You are hundreds of feet below sea level in the Afar Depression in Ethiopia. Two seas lie above you. They are widening because of plate movement. One day they may re-flood this African "Death Valley."

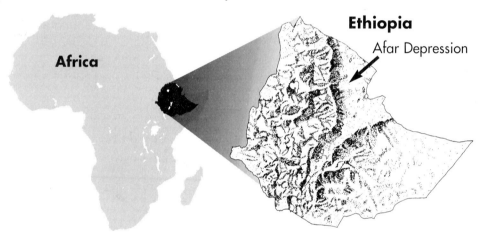

What's Your First Clue?

Small salt cones may be volcanic action at its gentlest. Gentle or not, volcano action makes itself felt. Or smelled. Or seen.

It sends signals. The trick is to read them right. And *right away!*

- Wells and springs may start to dry up.
- Flocks of birds fly away.
- Animals become very restless.
- Snakes slither into town from the mountain behind you.

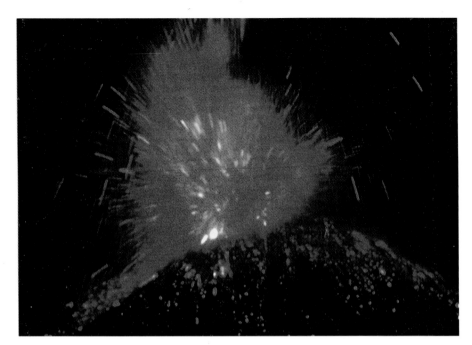

Parícutin in Mexico. This cinder cone volcano formed in a cornfield.

Surtsey is an island near the south coast of Iceland. It was created by a 3½-year eruption.

You might be plowing in your cornfield. You notice a crack in the earth. It begins to open up.

As it opens, it spits up smoke and ash. It begins to hiss. Small superhot rocks set fire to nearby trees. By the end of the week, this smoking, spitting cone is five stories high.

That's how Mexico's Parícutin volcano developed.

You might be traveling at sea. You notice huge clouds of steam rising from the surface of the water.

Your ship nears the cloud. Now you can hear the scream of steam and water roiling. The smell of sulfur makes your nose wrinkle. Small hot rocks the size of baseballs rain down. They hit your ship.

You see lumpy sprays of fiery red lava. They raise more steam clouds wherever they hit the water.

That's how Iceland's Surtsey Island started.

Volcano Islands

Volcano islands are underwater mountains whose tops poke out of the sea. They form from a buildup of cinders and ash. But the buildup must be protected by cooled lava. Otherwise, it can be washed away by ocean waves.

Some islands don't make it. Scientists watched an island start off the coast of Japan. The island would start. Then the ocean would wash it away. Now you see it. Now you don't. This happened over and over.

A ship with 22 men aboard went in for a closer look. It was at one of the "now you don't" see it times. Volcanic action chose that moment to make another attempt at an island.

Only a few pieces of wreckage from the boat were ever found. A few days later, the island, called Myozin, disappeared. For now, anyway.

Vent Variety

What do you see when you think of a volcano? A tall mountain with smoke coming out of the top?

The truth is, volcanoes come in many versions. There's the mountain version. There's the build-an-island version. And there's the hole-in-the-ground version through which steam rises.

The **vent,** or opening, might produce a **hot spring** or a bubbling mud pot. The vent might be a long crack, or **fissure,** in the ground. There might even be more than one vent per volcano.

Volcano Life Story

Volcanoes live very long lives. Hundreds of thousands of years. By comparison, human beings live short lives. So people don't have a chance to observe the "life story" of any particular volcano.

This can be a problem. It was at Vesuvius.

People had lived near Vesuvius for hundreds of years. But no one had ever recorded any stories about it being a volcano.

Besides, no one knew how to read the signals. For example, there had been earthquakes around Vesuvius for over ten years before 79 A.D. And months before the explosion, Vesuvius vented great clouds of smoke and ash.

Today, we know more about signals. Reading the signals helped when Mount St. Helens erupted in 1980.

But there are false warnings. Hawaii's Kilauea is a gentle volcano. And it vents lava almost all the time.

Still, it's best to heed the warnings. Better safe than sorry!

On the Watch

Today, we watch any volcano that has ever been recorded. Volcanoes that were active before records are also watched.

What is "active" for a volcano? Is it active when it only erupts once in 100 years? Or is it active when it erupts every seven years?

Hundreds of thousands of people all over the world live near volcanoes. Towns have grown up there. How do we know if a volcano is waking or if it is simply snoring?

Think About It

Mt. Everest is the world's highest peak at 29,002 feet. Mauna Kea in Hawaii is taller than Mt. Everest. But only 13,796 feet of its total 33,476 feet are above sea level.

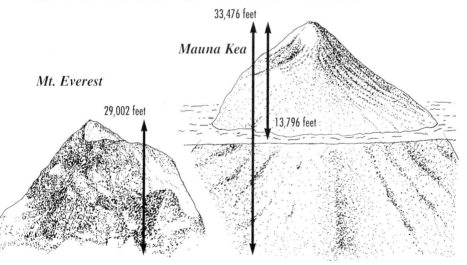

33,476 feet

Mauna Kea

Mt. Everest

29,002 feet

13,796 feet

Famous Exploration

Bruce Heezen was one of the first to observe the volcano rift running along the center of the mid-Atlantic ridge.

CHAPTER

Under Surveillance

Control, Watch, and Evacuation Plans

Imagine You clutch one suitcase in your hand. It is filled with all you can carry. You are about to leave the only home you've ever known.

A cinder cone rises at the edge of your fishing village. It is spewing hot ash and cinders. The hot ash covers streets and houses. It fills the harbor.

For two months, your island has shaken with tremors. Then the rock slides at the edge of town cut through a water pipe. A ground bubble started swelling at about five feet per hour.

One freezing September night, the bubble broke. In three days, white smoke, cinders, hot rocks, and spits of lava built up a cone.

So far, everyone is safe. Your father and others have talked with scientists thousands of miles away. They say everyone must leave the island before the volcano worsens. Boats will take you away.

Until then, you wait. But you worry about the growing dome at the edge of your village.

If this is 1961, you are standing on Tristan da Cunha. This is an island that lies between the bottom of South America and Africa. It's on the **mid-Atlantic ridge.**

The evacuated villagers lived in England for 18 months. The volcano destroyed the village's landing beach and part of the town. When the islanders returned, they cleaned up and rebuilt the island.

Making History

The first record of an erupting volcano was in 79 A.D. It was in a letter written by a Roman to his friend. This is how scientists learned that Vesuvius could explode. And bury towns.

The Roman wrote exactly what he could see, hear, and feel. His description matched the Mount St. Helens explosion in 1980. But the 1980 record was on videotape.

In Hawaii during the 1800s, a woman kept notebooks describing volcanic activity on land and sea. She wrote down dates and times, shapes, smells, and colors. Her notebooks captured over 50 years of information.

Scientists use these accounts. The records form part of the history of a volcano's very long life.

The accounts answer questions about a volcano's past activity. How did the volcano signal it would erupt? How much notice did it give before erupting?

Volcano Detectives

A *volcanologist* is a person who studies volcanoes. A volcano detective.

The volcanologist wants to measure everything.
- how hot lava is
- what volcanoes spit out

- when gases change
- how many times the earth quakes
- how much ice or water lies around the vent

Volcanoes can be classified by their shapes. There are four types. The shape offers the volcanologist clues about the kind of eruption to expect.

A **cinder cone volcano** looks like an upside-down ice-cream cone. Cinders and large heated rocks escape from the vent. They build a steep cinder mountain.

The cone is built quickly. But this volcano rarely grows much higher than 1,000 feet.

1971 eruption of Cerro Negro, in Nicaragua. Cerro Negro is a cinder cone volcano.

Mount St. Helens, in the Cascade Mountains in Washington State, erupts on May 18, 1980.

Ash, cinders, and larger, heated rocks escape from the vent of a **composite volcano.** Then lava escapes and covers the ash. More ash. More lava. Most volcanoes are this type.

Long periods of quiet usually mean the volcano is up to no good!

Thick magma pushes up beneath rock and soil to make a steep-sided dome shape, called a **dome volcano.** After an eruption, the volcano can become plugged with hardened lava. Gases build up until the volcano blows its top.

A **shield volcano** is wider than it is tall. Runny lava forms this wide mountain with gentle slopes.

The shield volcano is the "quiet type." It can produce a lot of lava that keeps building up on itself. Some examples are Mauna Loa and Mauna Kea (Hawaii), Emi Koussi (Africa), and Olympus Mons (Mars)—the largest known volcano in our solar system.

Olympus Mons   NASA

Dangerous Work

Volcano detectives have dangerous jobs. They enter active craters to take samples. They work at the edges of vents that could erupt at any moment. They move carefully along the top of cooling lava to record temperatures.

They face death by fire, by unseen gases, and by avalanches of fiery rock. All to advance our knowledge and help save lives.

Keeping Watch

Volcanologists study nature and use many kinds of equipment to monitor volcanoes.

Remote Sensing

Scanners make images of soft and solid areas up to 20 miles into the earth. They can find and measure magma moving underground.

Tilt!

A tiltmeter can measure swelling in the earth.

Lasers

Lasers bounce a light beam to a reflector and back to the light source. A computer times how long the light takes to make the round trip. It also measures any movement.

Gas Sampler

A gas sampler measures which gases are present. Airplanes can sample gases right over the vent. They look for a decrease in water vapor or an increase in sulfur. Both signal that an explosion may occur soon.

Rock Magnets

Heated rocks that are spit from the vent tell about what might happen. They are tested to measure their magnetism.

As the rocks get warmer, they lose their magnetic strength. So rocks with poor magnetic strength are signs that magma is on the move. And an eruption may soon take place.

Photographic Proof

Airplanes, satellites, and spacecraft take photos and computer-enhanced images. They may show small details like lava domes, opening fissures, or stampeding wildlife.

Water Wary

Volcanologists check groundwater and ice around a vent. Groundwater becomes steam when magma heats it. An eruption is more explosive with added steam power.

Thick areas of ice melt when hot ash and cinders roll over it. The mixture produces major mudflows. They can bury towns, valleys, and whole lakes!

Where Does the Flow Go?

Scientists study the volcano's surface. It helps them predict how ash, rocks, lava, or mud might flow down the slopes.

Are the slopes steep? Are there riverbed channels to carry the flow? Are there many natural curves that might slow or deflect danger?

Lava Footprints

Volcanologists test old magma. They study its elements.

Lava rich in potassium, silica, and sodium was thick when it erupted. Lava rich in iron and magnesium was runny.

Volcano detectives observe footprints in lava and ash from old eruptions. They learn what kind of damage was caused by past eruptions. And how much ground they covered.

Every eruption is different. But knowing what a volcano has done suggests what a new eruption might do.

DE-fense!

Volcanologists assist in emergency and evacuation plans. They design computer simulations to practice saving lives.

Scientists build special dams and **baffles.** The dams trap large boulders and slow mudflows that can kill people who live below.

The dams can't stop everything. But they give people more time to evacuate safely. This is used on some volcanoes in Japan.

People dig channels around some volcanoes. These channels divert lava flows away from cities and towns.

In Kagoshima, Japan, the whole town practices volcano drills. Across the bay is the volcano, Sakurajima.

A volcano is too powerful to stop. But we can predict how destructive an eruption might be. And when an eruption is likely to occur.

The best plan is to leave the volcano to blow its top. Then return when it calms down.

Living with volcanoes is tricky business. People in volcano areas need evacuation plans. They need to be ready when the volcano heats up.

Think About It

The Philippine volcano Mount Pinatubo erupted in 1991 and 1992. It had not erupted for 600 years. Volcanologists helped save 200,000 lives.

Mount Pinatubo in the Philippines—June 12, 1991

The eruptions of Mount Pinatubo killed nearly 900 people and buried valuable cropland. Enough to bury Miami, Florida, four times over.

Scientists observe a hot mudflow in the Sacobia Valley following the 1991 eruption of Mount Pinatubo.

Famous Volcanologists

Maurice and Katia Krafft were two of the most famous volcanologists. They were known as daredevils.

Wherever there was a volcano, they'd be there. And oftentimes, dangerously close!

The Kraffts took pictures of lava pouring down mountainsides. They photographed mud slowly burying everything in its path.

Their goal was to educate the 500 million people living in the shadows of dangerous volcanoes. They also wanted to help other volcanologists better understand this force of nature.

In 1991, Maurice and Katia Krafft were killed while filming the eruption of Mt. Unzen in Japan.

CHAPTER 4

Full Blast

Eruptions

Imagine You are piloting a 747. Suddenly, dust blows into the cockpit.

You look outside. You seem to be flying inside a cloud. But there shouldn't be clouds seven miles above the earth.

You smell sulfur. Is there a fire on board? You check your instruments.

Nothing shows on your radar. Your instruments and crew tell you there's no fire on board.

Then one of your four engines runs down. You shut it off. Soon, one engine after another has problems. You shut off the other three engines.

There are over 260 people aboard. What can you do in an airplane with no engines? How much time do you have?

You'll have to land the plane at sea. You try to guide the plane like a glider. But you're dropping almost 2,000 feet per second.

You keep trying to restart the engines. Only 2½ miles from the ground, the engines start.

What happened?

A volcano erupted. It spit up its fine ash and sulfur all around you. The hot ash cooled quickly around your engines and turned to glass. That clogged the air intake.

As you dropped from the heated air, the thin glass coatings shattered and blew from the engines. Then your engines restarted.

Thar She Blows!

Not all volcanoes create equal eruptions.

Cinder cone eruptions
- Magma is thick and slow-moving.
- Gases have trouble escaping.
- Pressure is released near the vent.
- Gases expand to explode lava into bits.
- Bits fall as ash and cinders.
- Cinders give way to larger heated rocks of every size.
- Lava runs down one of the cone's steep sides.
- The cone collapses under the weight of the lava.

Composite volcano eruptions
- Magma vibrates as it rises and expands upward.
- Steep cones collapse.
- Loose layers of ash, cinder, and rocks hold groundwater.
- Magma heats up the rock, often to melting.
- Magma also heats the water to steam.
- Steam increases the magma's speed with its own explosive energy.
- Steam produces a frothy magma that splatters.

Sometimes old plugs of material from the last eruption block the vent. So the magma finds a weak spot in the wall of the volcano and fills it. From the outside, a dome grows. Or ash, cinders, and larger heated rocks race down the slopes in glowing avalanches.

This happened to the north face of Mount St. Helens in 1980. Breaking loose, the rock ripped down the mountain at 200 mph. It crashed into a lake, over a ridge, and down almost 17 miles into a river valley.

It was the largest landslide in recorded history. And the eruption was just starting!

Lava dome eruptions

- Domes bulge with hot and expanding magma.
- Lava flow is thick and travels only a short distance.
- The edges of the flow cool in a crust.
- The crust breaks up into blocks.
- Blocks are pushed along by the hotter lava beneath.

Shield volcano eruption

- Magma gases expand near the surface of the volcano.
- Runny lava is propelled from the vent.
- Lava forms rivers or collects in fiery lakes.

November 27, 1989. Molten lava from Kalapana, Hawaii, forms a river.

- Eruptions are not violent, but they are frequent.
- Shield volcanoes build on themselves.
- They become massive mountains.

Shield volcanoes erupt like soda fizzing from a pop bottle. When you pop the cap, you hear a hiss. The hiss is the carbon dioxide gas expanding. Popping the cap releases the pressure.

Cover the open top with your thumb. Shake the soda. What happens? A soda eruption. So much gas is released that it propels the soda right out of the bottle.

Explosive Eruptions

Scientists divide eruptions into different types. A volcano may have more than one type of eruption.

Hawaiian/Icelandic

These eruptions are named after the places where they generally occur. They range from a drool to a fountain of fluid lava. As eruptions go, these are "quiet."

1951 eruption of Stromboli

Strombolian

This type is named after the volcano on the island of Stromboli, Italy. Stromboli is called "The Lighthouse of the Mediterranean."

Stromboli erupts often. It bubbles and spits runny lava fragments. They settle around the vent to build up its crater.

28

Vesuvian

This type is named after Vesuvius, which erupted in 79 A.D. A column of fragments rises at least 12½ miles high in a great umbrella-shaped cloud. As it spreads, the cloud rains ash.

Then the column collapses back around the vent. The superheated material charges down the mountain in glowing avalanches.

This photo of Lassen Peak in California was taken 33 km from the 1915 eruption.

How Hot Is That Color?

The color of lava tells us about its temperature. The hotter the lava, the more easily it flows.

**hottest
lava at vent
is white (upwards
from 2,200° F)**

begins to cool and yellow (around 2,000° F)

orange (around 1,650° F)

bright red (about 1,290° F)

dark red (around 930° F)

begins to turn solid and gray or black

December 3, 1982. Lightning strikes at Galunggung,
Indonesia, during a volcanic eruption.

Lava from Mauna Ulu in Hawaii consumes vegetation—
January 25, 1974.

Special Effects

Lightning often occurs during an eruption. You will see it at the bottom of the ash cloud rising in the sky.

The tiny ash particles in the cloud rub against one another. This produces massive charges of static electricity.

The electricity is released as lightning. It twists around in the ash cloud from charge to charge like white yarn.

Tips on How to Defend Your Village

The people on the island of Heimaey, Iceland, offer the following tips.

1. Remove all vehicles and boats from the path of the volcano.
2. Clean ash from roofs. Do this often. Ash is heavy, and too much will collapse a roof.
3. Douse fires lit by hot fragments.
4. Place corrugated sheet metal over windows. This will keep hot fragments from breaking in and setting fire to the inside of your house.
5. Hose off the wings of aircraft.
6. Keep the runway cleared for emergency landings and takeoffs.
7. Flood the leading edges of lava flows with cold seawater to slow them down.

This plane is covered with ash from the June 1991 eruption of Mt. Pinatubo.

Famous Observations

Pliny the Younger wrote the first reports of an erupting volcano—Vesuvius.

CHAPTER 5

Faster Than the Speed of Sound

Speed and Destruction

Imagine You are in a jail cell. Suddenly, you hear a terrible earth-rattling roar. The ground is shaking. You fight to stay on your feet.

You open your mouth to scream. But you can't hear your own voice. The sound outside deafens you. It sounds like thousands of steam locomotives.

You stagger back against the bars of your cell. It hurts to breathe. Your chest is heavy and sore.

The air is foul. You cover your nose with your shirt. Then a tremendous explosion rocks the jail. You fall to the floor.

An invisible wave of heat floods through your cell. Your skin burns. You are too scared to move. What can you do?

You are hurt. And you can't live without food or water. You prepare to die.

Four days later you are rescued. After your injuries are treated, you venture outside.

You can hardly believe your eyes. As far as you can see, only the bottoms of buildings are left.

Everyone in the town has been killed. You are the only survivor.

What has happened?

If this is 1902, you are on the island of Martinique. You are viewing what's left of Saint-Pierre. And there isn't much.

All caused by Mount Pelée. And it only took 2½ minutes!

Dangerous Stuff

Gases

Gases mix, expand, and separate from the magma to cause an eruption. This mix helps determine the explosive power of the eruption.

Sulfur dioxide and hydrogen sulfide are often present. They announce themselves with a rotten-egg smell.

Chlorine, fluorine, and/or sulfur make breathing difficult. These gases can irritate or damage eyes and lungs. They can also eat through unprotected clothing.

Carbon dioxide is hard to detect. It has no smell. It is also heavy and can collect in basements and small valleys. There it can suffocate unsuspecting animal life—from mice to humans.

Lava

Remember, when magma reaches the surface, it is called lava. Sudden eruptions are common with runny magma. Gases that are present expand as the magma rises. This produces a froth that cools in the air. Then it falls as a light rock called **pumice.**

Violent eruptions usually occur with thick magma. Thick magma holds fewer gases. And these gases expand beneath the thick magma. The resulting explosion shatters or blows out rock into smaller pieces.

In a long-lasting eruption, runny lava may flow at any speed up to about 31 mph. As it cools, lava slows down.

The lava cools on the surface. But it may continue to flow beneath the crust.

A lava flow is slow enough for people to avoid. So it rarely causes death. But it can travel great distances, covering roads and destroying crops and buildings in its path.

In different places around the world, people have tried to slow lava. They have pumped cold water on its edges. Or placed barriers in its way. Some have even tried to change its path with explosives.

June 21, 1989. Volunteers spray water on advancing lava at the Wahaula Visitor Center in Hawaii.

Ash

Smaller pieces of lava are called ash, or dust. A thin layer of ash can add nutrients to soil. During some Hawaiian eruptions, people drive up to collect bags of ash for their gardens or farms.

Too much ash destroys crops. It collapses roofs, clogs water systems, impairs breathing, and hinders transportation. It gets into engines and chokes machinery.

Water

Groundwater is heated by rising magma. It changes to steam.

Steam pressure adds to explosive power. It can expand itself a thousandfold in seconds. Steam mixes well with ash, cinders, and gases. This increases a volcano's destructive range.

This happened at Mount St. Helens. The expanding steam cloud overtook the rock landslide, traveling faster than the speed of sound!

Often water is added outside the vent. It comes in the form of rain, snow, ice, or streams, lakes, and rivers.

Mixing with ash, water can create rivers of mud. They are like a giant pour of cement, flowing as fast as 62 mph. Mudflows can fill lakes and valleys for dozens of miles.

The heat inside a volcano can melt snow and ice on its slopes. This is what happened on November 13, 1985, on Nevado del Ruiz in Colombia.

The melted water headed down the mountain. On its way, it stripped all soils and ash in its path. This produced a mud river the size of a 13-story building. It traveled about 25 mph. It engulfed the town of Amero, 30 miles away. And over 20,000 of its people.

Bombs

During an eruption, unexploded lava or loose rock can be hurled from the crater around the vent. These superheated pieces, called **bombs,** range in size from baseballs to buildings. They can set fire to vegetation or houses wherever they hit the ground. They can also crush or injure animal life.

Glowing avalanches

After some time, erupted ash and rock fall back around the volcano's top. Then they flow over the land in all directions. They form a glowing avalanche.

This avalanche of superheated material races down the mountain. It travels at hurricane speed and force. Temperatures range up to 1,500° F.

Sometimes gravity breaks the avalanche into two parts—**surge** and flow. The surge is a dark gray cloud of superheated fine ash. It separates from the heavier material. Then it surges ahead.

This surge scorches, shreds, and sandblasts anything in its way. It travels at speeds from 62–186 mph, reaching temperatures around 212° F. The surge billows out and up on its own currents of heat and expanding gases.

Following right behind is the flow. This is the heavier, ground-hugging rush of superheated material. The flow mows down anything left standing. It travels at speeds from 12½ to 31 mph and at temperatures around 752° F.

Eroded mountainside and steam cloud following 1980 eruption of Mount St. Helens

The Biggest, Baddest Boomers

Engraving of 1866 eruption of Nea Kameni, Santorini, Greece

Thera • Santorini Island, Greece • 1500 B.C.

An earthquake triggered the eruption. The ash was up to 200 feet high in places. Thera started a series of huge sea waves traveling up to 200 mph.

The ash and the waves sank fleets of ships and clogged harbors. Thera's power smashed towns and buried palaces. It formed a sea basin so deep that no ship could ever again anchor in it.

The destruction of this island probably started the Atlantis legend. Thera is slowly rebuilding itself.

Tambora • Sumbawa Island, Indonesia • 1815

The eruption killed 12,000 people. Another 80,000 starved to death because their crops and livestock were destroyed.

Tambora released 40 times more ash into the atmosphere than Mount St. Helens.

Krakatoa • in the Sundra Strait near the Indonesian island of Java • August 26 and 27, 1883

Crews on ships 17 miles away shoveled ash from decks to avoid sinking. The next day, the volcano collapsed on itself.

The force of the eruption created a ten-story wave. The wave swept away almost 300 towns and killed over 30,000 people.

Katmai • Alaska, USA • June 6, 1912

The earthquake started giving signals around June 1. A mountain face collapsed. This set off a hurricane of dust and rock for 15 miles.

Then a new vent opened six miles from the top of the volcano. From vent to valley, columns of glowing ash erupted. The ash covered the earth up to 700 feet thick in places.

Drawing of Krakatoa ash cloud

The vent at the top of Katmai started to erupt. But it collapsed in on itself. Then the new vent really started to cook.

For 2½ days, it spewed out ash and rock 25 miles into the **stratosphere.** Ash fell for three days in Kodiak, a two-hour drive from Katmai.

When the eruption stopped, the new vent plugged itself. The raised valley floor steamed from thousands of fissures.

Think About It

No man-made bomb has come close to the explosive power of volcanoes. The atomic bomb that was dropped on Hiroshima caused an explosion equal to 19,000 tons of TNT.

The explosive power of some famous eruptions is shown on the next page.

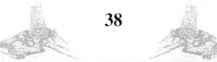

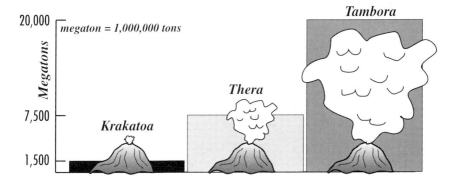

megaton = 1,000,000 tons

Megatons: 20,000 — 7,500 — 1,500

Tambora

Thera

Krakatoa

Famous Exploration

Volcanologists measure the temperature of lava before, during, and after eruptions. One important tool they use is an **infrared scanner.**

Infrared radiation is light given off by heat. Warm objects emit more radiation than cool objects. Infrared scanners can detect this radiation. And if the lava is heating up…

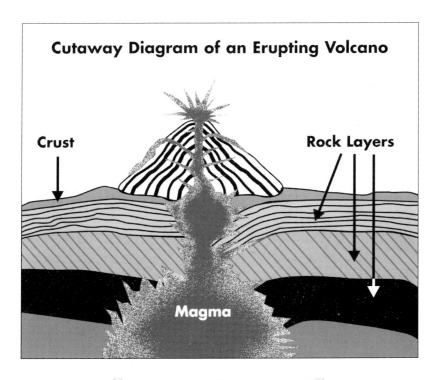

Cutaway Diagram of an Erupting Volcano

Crust

Rock Layers

Magma

CHAPTER

Just When You Think It's Over

Aftermath

Imagine You stand at the edge of a Nebraska cornfield. Looking down into a gully, you can't believe your eyes. Below you is a gleaming white skull. It is trapped in the wall of the old streambed.

Gently, carefully, you pick it up. You brush away the gray ash around the bone.

It doesn't look like a horse or cow skull. And it's not big enough to be a dinosaur skull. Too bad.

You are surprised to find that it is still attached to its neck bones. Could a whole fossil lie behind the neck bones? It does!

Scientists have dug up dozens of complete fossil skeletons. They have found elephants, three-toed horses, camels, birds, mice, lizards, and turtles! Even rhinoceros fossils!

How did they get here? When? What happened to them?

It was ten million years ago when some distant volcano vented ash. The ash overcame the animals at their small watering hole.

The animals suffocated on the glass-sharp ash as they tried to breathe. They died slow deaths.

What Is Left—and Right?

The aftermath of an eruption has many parts.

Ash

Ash and cinders usually stay on the ground where they fall. A thick layer of ash can mix with rainfall to produce mudflows that cause more damage. But thinner layers can mix with snow or rain and nourish the soil.

Lava

Lava creates more land. But it stays hot for years.

In some cases, lava runs into the sea. The sudden cold breaks it up into grains of black glass. This produces black sand beaches.

Most volcanoes live under the sea. Here the lava often erupts in small amounts at a time. It builds up around the volcano in piles called pillow lava.

Caldera

Often, part of the volcano collapses into a space without magma. This creates a basin in the ground called a *caldera.*

Sometimes the top of a volcano seems to vanish. The remaining caldera eventually fills with water to become a lake. There are many caldera lakes around the world.

Mount Mazama was a volcano that blew itself up in 4600 B.C. The eruption charred trees 35 miles away. Most of the mountain vanished. About $\frac{1}{10}$ was spit out in the eruption. The remaining $\frac{9}{10}$ collapsed into its own empty magma chamber.

The collapse made a caldera 6 miles wide and 4,000 feet deep. Today, this caldera is known as Crater Lake, Oregon.

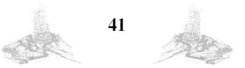

41

When an island volcano collapses, all that remains is the outside edge. Some island calderas are so big they have become part of the sea. What was once a volcano island may now appear as a broken ring of islands.

Lake in a caldera in Taal, Philippines— September 1965

Cones

Cones built too steep during an eruption will start to settle. As the new rock settles, the older rock may not be strong enough to hold it up. Rock falls will send small avalanches down the slopes.

Sometimes an entire mountain face will fall. It can become a huge avalanche. For miles, it cuts down anything in its path.

Gas

Large releases of ash and sulfur dioxide can spread high through our atmosphere. This reduces the solar energy reaching earth.

Less heat from the sun means lower temperatures. Harvests may be poorer than usual. Crops may fail.

In 1816, Tambora's eruption caused the "year with no summer." Snow fell on North America from June through August. There were early frosts, poor crops, and food shortages in Europe.

People Problems

When land is covered or destroyed, it's not just houses, crops, and livestock that are lost. People are affected too.

Even when people are evacuated safely, they must have somewhere to go. Most governments work to arrange shelter and help for their people.

If your city were suddenly destroyed by a volcano, where could you go? How would you find a place to live? Clean clothes to wear? Food to eat? If you were separated from your family, how could you find them?

Right after an eruption, there is much confusion. Communications may be cut off. Roads, rivers, railways, and even airstrips may be destroyed or clogged. So rescue workers, food, and other supplies cannot arrive.

The Mount Pinatubo eruption on June 12, 1991, caused an ash buildup 1–2 meters high within a 3 kilometer area.

Rescue workers are not the only ones working hard after an eruption. Volcanologists continue risking their lives.

They take samples from the still-smoldering ash or lava. They continue monitoring from airplanes and satellites. Everything is examined to learn more about the eruption.

How Volcanoes Tell Tales

Volcanic ash and flows have advanced our understanding of life on earth. They capture skeletons of animals that lived many millions of years ago. They record what kind of eruption took place and how long it lasted.

There are cultures that disappeared before there were historical records. But volcanoes provide their own historical records.

When Vesuvius erupted in 79 A.D., it covered whole cities. Two of the cities destroyed were Herculaneum and Pompeii.

In the remains of Herculaneum, human skeletons were found buried in ash wet from centuries of rain. The wet mud preserved the skeletons. Bits of clothing and many of the objects people carried as they fled were also found.

In Pompeii, people suffocated in the first gas surge that blasted through the town. The flow that followed hardened around each body.

Soft body parts decayed, but the forms remained. These forms showed body shape, facial expression, and clothing details. Plaster casts have been made of these "ghost" cavities.

These ruins were discovered almost 300 years ago. And the digging continues today. Much of what we know about this time is still being discovered in these towns.

Famous Connection

Benjamin Franklin was the first observer to link volcano ash clouds to climate change.

CHAPTER 7

Going for Green

Cleanup

Imagine You've spent six months on the mainland waiting for the eruption to stop. You have just returned to the island.

Half of your fishing village is covered to the rooftops in ash and cinders. More than 400 homes have been destroyed. The town's main industry lies buried under lava.

All you can see is a village covered in ash. Even the fields are covered. The hills behind the buried part of town used to be so green. Now they are covered in ash too.

A bulldozer digs out the streets. People clean and repair the houses still standing. Your father and mother work all day with other adults to build new houses.

But what can you do? At school you discuss what might be done. Soon you are helping to clean up the village.

You and your friends shovel off the loose ash and cinders from the hills. You toss each shovelful onto a chute that loads the trucks below.

The trucks take away this nutrient-rich gravel. It will be exported from the island.

You look for warm rocks that are too thick to remove. Then

you scatter hay and grass seed over them. The hay will decay in the heat and speed up seed growth.

For the next few summers, you and your friends will rescue the hills! When you finish, the hills will be green again.

If it is 1973, you are on the island of Heimaey in Iceland.

What's the Plan?

After an eruption, people develop a plan. Whatever can be saved or repaired will be.

Land buried under lava, rock slides, and mudflows stays buried. New roads are built over or around damaged areas. Some are rerouted.

Rivers are dredged of ash and rock. This deepens them to let ships through. Some of the felled trees are saved as lumber.

New tracks are laid for railways. Electric power, telephone, and water lines are fixed. Flood controls, mud dams, and rock traps may be built to help reduce future damage.

Sometimes a park marks the area. It becomes a place where people can study volcanoes. And learn about the environment and how it recovers from destruction. Postage stamps, songs, postcards, T-shirts, and stickers record some volcano events.

Nature Heals Itself

Nature works on its own to rebuild. Insects and small animals may still live in burrows. These small creatures can survive in the bases of trees that are knocked over.

When the heat dies down, larger animals move back in. They root through ash and broken vegetation.

Seeds are carried in by animals, visiting birds, and air currents. Hardy weeds and grasses will push up through ash that is not too deep.

New plant growth on a cold lava flow in Hawaii

Lava from a Hawaiian volcano creates new beach areas.

Bacteria and molds join insects and other animals to break up decaying vegetation. Berries, bracken fern, and fireweed are often some of the first to reappear.

Waves bring new life to volcano islands. They carry algae, mussels, rushes, and seaweed.

Left on their own, even lakes recover. Spirit Lake is a good example. In 1993, this beautiful lake in the Cascades held more **plankton** and nutrients than before Mount St. Helens erupted in 1980. That was 13 years after it was smothered with ash and broken trees.

Rock Heaven

Volcanoes produce interesting rocks. So rock collectors like to visit eruption sites too. There are rocks with small crystals that are formed as the lava cools.

Pumice develops when gas bubbles are trapped inside a cooling lava particle. These pebbles float like corks. They can be cut with a knife.

Pumice

Some people look for diamonds. They will sift through cinders for days.

But volcanoes don't spit out diamonds. The diamonds always turn out to be fragments of crystal-bright quartz.

Rock crystal with pyrite

Lava that cools very quickly has no time to form tiny crystals. It cools as glassy **black obsidian.** This is used for arrowheads and cutting tools.

Obsidian rocks that freeze as drops are called Pelé's Tears. If they freeze as threads, they are called Pelé's Hair. Pelé is the Hawaiian volcano goddess.

Obsidian

CHAPTER 8

The Power Behind the Stone

Harnessing Volcano Product

Imagine You help your parents dig a small pit to cook your birthday dinner. Your aunts, uncles, and cousins are coming. There will be so many people!

So much food! It took the three of you to carry it all. You have chosen to have cozido, a family favorite.

You cram beef, chicken, pork, sausage, kale, and other vegetables into metal pots. Then you wrap and tie large clean cloths around each pot.

The pots will keep the sulfur fumes from touching the food. The long ends of the cloths will help you carry the steaming pots home.

Your mother thinks it will take many hours to cook so much food. For your oven, you dig an "eight-hour" hole.

You bury the pots in the hot earth about 8 a.m. As the foods heat, the juices will slowly blend together. The meat will be perfect. The vegetables steamed. All cooked by the hot earth near the lake. The entire feast will be ready at 4 p.m.

The hot earth you're using is near Lake Furnas in the Azore Islands. The Azores are part of the mid-Atlantic ridge. Lake Furnas is the caldera of an active volcano.

What a Place to Live!

Why do people live near volcanoes? Why do people return to volcanoes after an eruption? Are they crazy or what?

People return to volcano areas because of the good things. For example, volcanoes add more land to live on. More soil.

Cinder and composite volcanoes produce elements that enrich soils. Around deadly Vesuvius is soil that grows grains, grapes, and olives. As many as *four* vegetable crops a year.

In the fields around Indonesian and Philippine volcanoes, you can harvest three full rice crops a year. Coconuts, mangoes, yams, potatoes, bananas, peanuts, and corn are also grown.

Pick a volcano, pick a crop. From limes to lettuce. From timber to tobacco.

Some ash is an important part of cement, waterproof mortar, and insulation. Lava is often dug for building materials.

Volcanoes are also tourist attractions. Lovely to look at. And look out from. Many national parks feature volcano activity.

Sometimes the energy that fuels volcano action can be harnessed.

In Hot Water

When groundwater is heated by magma, it rises to the surface. Where this water collects is called a hot spring. This heated water contains many minerals.

Sometimes hot water and steam struggle to the surface at the same time. Traveling through a narrow exit, this mixture produces a **geyser.**

A geyser erupts with built-up pressure. Then it dies down until the next buildup of pressure.

There are also hot sands and hot mud. For thousands of years, people living nearby have bathed in them. They believe they are good for the skin.

Heat Energy

Energy produced by the earth's inner heat is called **geothermal energy.** *Geo* means "earth" and *therme* means "heat." Around the world, more people are putting geothermal energy to work.

Water is always sinking into the earth. It comes from rain and melting snow or ice. There it joins the water that is already underground.

Water caught near a pocket of magma heats up. If the water heats up quickly, it turns to steam.

Steam takes up more space than water. So with this added pressure, the steam rises back up through the earth. If there is enough steam pressure, it often escapes through the crust of the earth.

A deep vent where steam rises is called a *fumarole.* There are many fumaroles around the world. People near fumaroles have cooked over them for hundreds of years.

Fumaroles also heat water. In Deception Bay, Antarctica, fumaroles heat water to about 100° F. That means you can

bathe outdoors. But wear a hat to keep falling snow off your head!

Iceland sits on the mid-Atlantic ridge. The water under Iceland's ground is hot. There are hot springs, fumaroles, and geysers everywhere.

You can bathe and wash clothes in the hot springs. You can make small baking or slow-cooking ovens in the ground.

In Iceland's capital city, most buildings are heated with the geothermal water. This water is carried by pipes. Much like the way water comes into your school.

People in Iceland use geothermal energy to heat large greenhouses. There they grow flowers and fresh foods like bananas, tomatoes, cucumbers, and grapes. All on the Arctic Circle!

Engineers use geothermal energy to run generators that produce electricity. You can find these in California, Italy, Mexico, New Zealand, Japan, Russia, and the Philippines.

 ## *Famous Park*

Yellowstone became the first national park in the world on March 1, 1872. Yellowstone's landscape was shaped by volcanoes and glaciers millions of years ago.

A major eruption occurred in the area about 2,000,000 years ago. Then 600,000 years ago, there was another eruption. Lava flows created plateaus that make up the Yellowstone landscape.

A huge crater 40 miles long and 30 miles wide was also formed. Yellowstone Lake is in part of this crater.

CHAPTER 9

What's the future?

Imagine You are in your lab on Space Station Freedom. You are on watch.

You place a new crystal into an infrared scanner. It will find areas on earth with high heat.

You locate dry, hot rock that can be used to heat water. You discover volcanoes heating up deep inside. Time to beam down a warning.

Then you continue. What about Venus? Is Beta Regio ready to erupt? Is it a danger to astronauts orbiting Venus?

What about that computer program you finished yesterday? Has it restarted the gas collector probe in orbit around Io, Jupiter's volcanic moon?

It's sometime in the 21st century. You have learned a great deal about earth's volcanoes. Already you have saved lives.

You are also helping people use volcano resources to improve their lives on earth. And ensure their safety as they explore earth's neighborhood.

Glossary

ash
soft, fine pieces of lava spit out by an erupting volcano

baffles
obstacles that slow or divert mudflows and large rocks away from people living below a mountain

black obsidian
dark, glassy volcanic rock formed by the rapid cooling of lava

bombs
superheated chunks of lava or rock spit out by an erupting volcano. They range in size from lemons to lighthouses.

caldera
huge crater that is formed when a volcano collapses

cinder cone volcano
a volcano that builds a steep mountain of cinders and other burnt rock around its vent. Sometimes part of the cone breaks away under its own weight and is as dangerous as the volcanic action itself.

composite volcano
rock fragments and lava erupt from a central vent to form this type of volcano. Most volcanoes are this type.

core
the center of planet earth. The inner core is packed solid under the pressure of a lot of weight. The outer core is a melted down or molten area heated by the inner core.

dome volcano
a volcano that builds a rounded mountain of rock and soil that sometimes bursts open, letting thick lava ooze out

fissure
a long, narrow crack in earth's crust

fumarole
a small, deep vent on or near a volcano through which steam rises

geothermal energy
heat energy produced inside earth. As steam or hot water, this energy may be used for large heating systems or for producing electricity.

geyser
a volcanic jet or fountain of water and steam

hot spots
fractures in earth's mantle, probably caused by meteorites punching right through earth's crust. The mantle vents magma through these hot spots.

hot spring	a small collection of mineral waters heated by underground magma from 70° F (21° C) upwards
infrared scanner	a tool that measures radiation given off by heat
lava	magma that has escaped from the volcano onto the earth's surface
magma	thick, molten rock that moves underground. When magma escapes to earth's surface, it is called lava.
mantle	the molten rock and gas covering earth's core. Earth's crust "rides" on the mantle.
meteorites	meteor fragments not completely destroyed in the fall to earth
mid-Atlantic ridge	a long, undersea mountain range built by volcanic action as two plates spread apart
plankton	very small animal and plant life found in water
plates	the great broken pieces of earth's crust that move slowly on the molten mantle
pumice	a light rock made from the froth of exploding, runny magma. It cools quickly with air bubbles trapped inside.
rift	a deep valley between earth's plates
Ring of Fire	the active volcanoes on the edges of the plates surrounding the Pacific Ocean. Over 75% of earth's land volcanoes are found here.
shield volcano	a volcano that builds a gently sloping, very wide mountain of runny lava
stratosphere	the portion of earth's atmosphere that begins approximately 7 miles (11 km) above earth's surface
surge	a strong, deadly volcanic cloud of superheated ash and gases that rushes ahead of the heavier flow of a glowing avalanche
vent	magma's escape route or exit from inside earth. Vents occur around the edges of earth's plates.

Index